A Book of Flies
Real
or
Otherwise

Poems and text by Richard Michelson
Drawings by Leonard Baskin

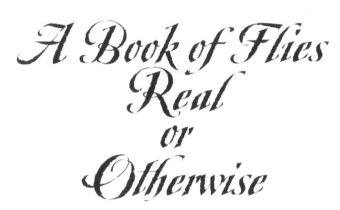

MARSHALL CAVENDISH   *New York*

A Book of Flies

Millions of years before there were jets, before there were bats, before there were birds, insects were the first to fly. And now, 300 million years of test flights later, flies are a success. They can swoop, loop, change direction, fly backwards or upside down. The common house fly can flap its wings two hundred times a second. Try flapping your arms that fast while hanging upside down.

More than eight out of every ten animals are insects. All insects belong to one of approximately twenty-six clubs (scientists call them orders). The bees are in one club, the ants join another. All true flies join the club we call Diptera. (In Greek, this means "two wings.") To join you have to have six legs and two wings.

If an insect has four wings, we might think it's a fly and even call it a fly, but it can never join the club Diptera. Sawflies, mayflies, and butterflies all have their own clubs.

There are close to 90,000 different "species" of flies. This book looks at nine of them (and four nonflies). You can make up your own poems for the 89,991 others. All flies are hatched from eggs into legless "larvae" called maggots. They are wingless and wormlike before they grow up and "earn their wings." Adult female flies can lay a lot of eggs at one time (imagine having a hundred brothers and sisters), and each grows up quickly. That's why there are so many flies.

If two flies mated in April and all their descendants lived, there would be 200,000,000,000,000,000,000 new flies by the end of the summer. Of course, I might have missed a couple. If you count them, and I'm wrong, please let me know.

Some female flies bite and suck blood (which helps them produce their eggs), and other flies carry and spread disease, but the vast majority of flies are harmless and they help us survive. They pollinate flowers and they're an important link in the food chain, serving as supper for birds and bats and many other animals. Flies also eat and bury dead animals, which helps keep the earth a little tidier.

Think about all that the next time you swat a fly.

Fruit Fly

If flies tasted like

I wouldn't feel so nauseous.
I have a hunch
next time I lunch
I'll be a bit more cautious.

'Cause I just ate a fruit fly
that was swimming in my cup.
I took a drink
and now I think
I'm going to throw up.

Fruit flies look like teeny-weeny house flies (ten of them, head to tail, would line up in less space than an inch). They have red eyes. Are they drunk? Well, they are also called wine flies, as they like alcohol and are often found in bars, where they settle on the rims of glasses, and occasionally get a little tipsy and tumble in. But they are just as likely to be found in health food stores, where they sample the organic fruits.

Scientists study fruit flies more than any other animal. That's because they grow and breed quickly so we can see what characteristics they pass down to their offspring. A mother fruit fly might lay twenty-five eggs a day for forty-five days in a row, and ask for nothing but a rotten bit of banana to eat. Her children will be full-grown in two weeks, the females ready to lay their own eggs. Scientists can watch everything they do in their entire lives, so don't complain the next time your parents ask what you've been up to.

Horse Fly

At first when I saw horses fly
I thought it SUPER DOOPER.
But SPLAT!!!
I should have worn a hat
and brought a pooper scooper.

If I were King I'd change some things:
I'd keep all horse flies chained
unless they wore cloth diapers or
were fully potty-trained.

Horse flies are huge flies (some as large as an inch long with a 2-inch wingspan) that feed on the blood of animals, especially . . . you guessed it, horses. Or at least the females do. The males prefer a flower's nectar.

Like horses, horse flies are often brown or gray in color, but they have speckled wings that, at rest, rest on each other like the roof of a house. They have a loud hmmmmmmmmmm when they fly, and although they don't carry diseases, their bite can sting like a wasp's, which is why horses swat at them with their tails.

Soldier Fly

The human being's a violent race.
They specialize in slaughter.

They'll use sweet-smelling sticky stuff.
They'll drown you in tap water.

They've engineered a death machine
for flies they call The Swatter.

They chased my sister 'round the room
and SLAPPED . . .
. . . until they got her.

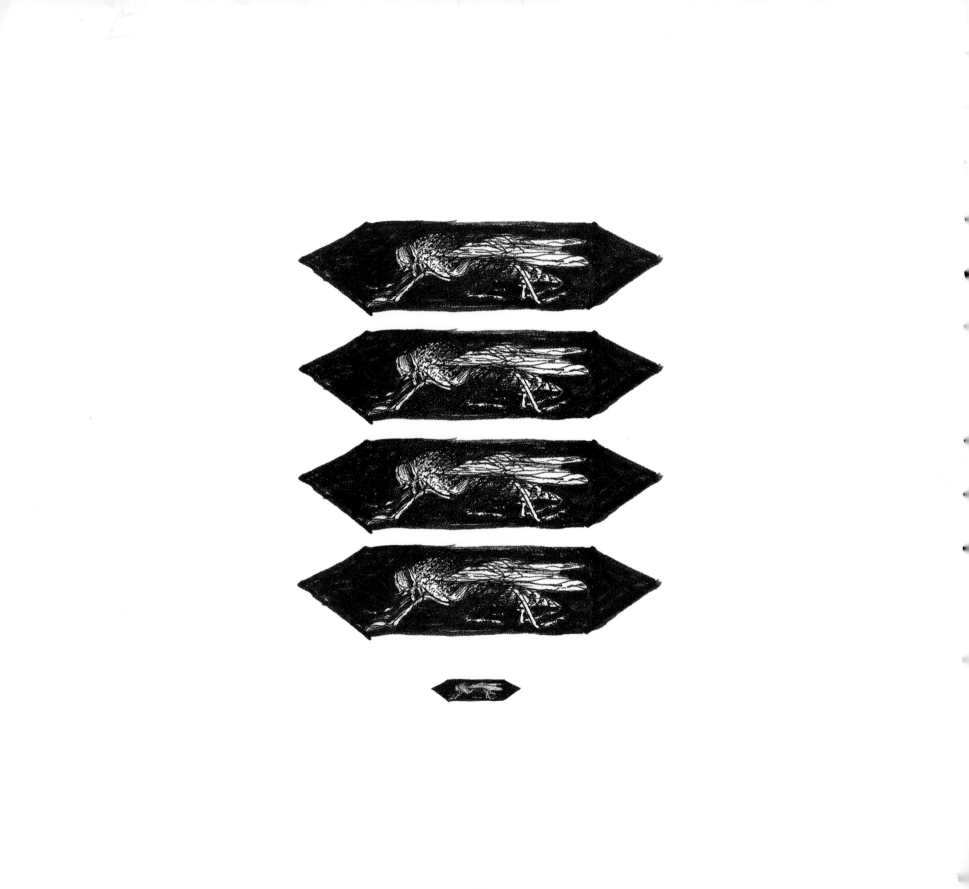

With its metallic-colored "uniform" and habit of resting with its wings held stiff and parallel over its back, the *Soldier fly* looks as though it has joined the military, but it acts more like a soldier on leave. Most of its time is spent resting on plants and sunning itself in gardens.

Since soldier flies are small and inactive, they do not create enough body heat to operate even their own wing muscles, so they depend on sunny conditions for flight. The wise General had best attack at midday. The troops will lose their power as the sun sets.

Firefly

The signs say:

> TODAY'S MATINEES
> ARE SOLD OUT.

The less mature children
throw tantrums and pout.
But I know I'll see any flick
that I pick
because my firefly has a failure-proof trick.

She waits till an usher or two rushes by her
then flashes her belly
until they yell
FIRE!!!

The crowds dash for exits.
My fly and I enter,
discreetly buy treats
and find seats
front
and
center.

Fireflies are neither flies (they are beetles), nor "on fire" but they really do flash a brilliant light. Like the corner stoplight, this can be either red, green, or yellow. Most females are unable to fly, and they flash their lights to attract males, which flash back in answer.

The firefly has a light-producing chemical stored in its stomach, which unlike our inefficient lightbulbs, creates light without heat, so the firefly doesn't burn up inside.

Fireflies can be collected and enclosed in paper lanterns for nighttime reading. You can even tangle them in your hair, before a late-night stroll. But do release them before you go to sleep.

Dragonfly

A damselfly,
demure and shy,
was pleading for her life.

A gallant knightfly
heard her cry
and swore she'd be his wife.

A dragonfly
was breathing flames.
Damsel was terrified.

"My love,"
the knight cried out.
Too late!
(for this hot date)
The dragon ate
her—fried.

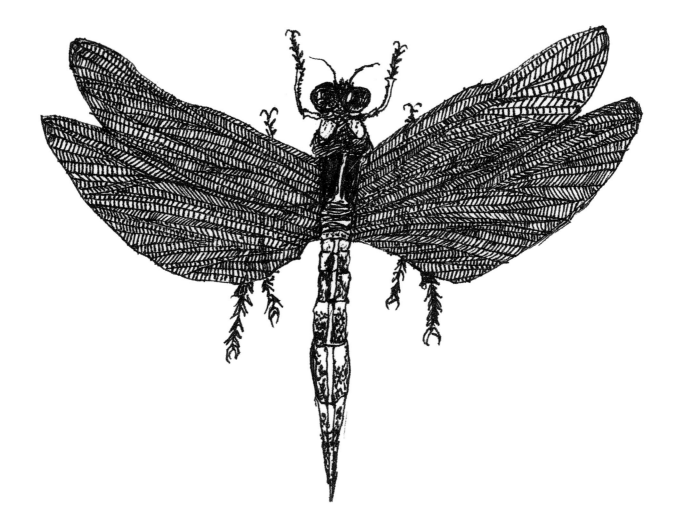

In the days of King Arthur and the Knights of the Round Table, Damsels were young women of noble birth, slender and elegant and always needing rescuing. The *Damselfly* is among the most beautiful of insects, but its flight is weak and fluttering. The *Dragonfly* is generally larger than the damselfly, and it is among the most powerful and fastest of fliers, sometimes reaching speeds of 60 miles per hour. At rest, its wings stretch straight out at its sides, daring you to enter its territory.

Dragonflies are virtually unchanged since prehistoric times, when they shared the earth with dinosaurs. Some were larger then (with 3-foot wingspans, ancient dragonflies were the largest flying insects of all time), but even today they have enormous eyes. While they don't literally breathe fire, dragonflies are fierce hunters whose prey had better not wait for a knightfly in shining armor to rescue them. Knightflies don't really exist.

Neither dragonflies nor damselflies are true flies. Both have two pairs of long narrow wings (true flies have one pair) and they belong to the order Odonata.

Mydas Fly

I'm Mydas Fly.

I'm filthy rich.

I'm wealthier than queens and kings.

The problem is my gold's no good.

Flies can't buy cars

or diamond rings.

Flies don't watch movies

or TV.

Flies don't wear clothes

(or underwear).

Our food is free.

O, woe is me.

I'm one unhappy millionaire.

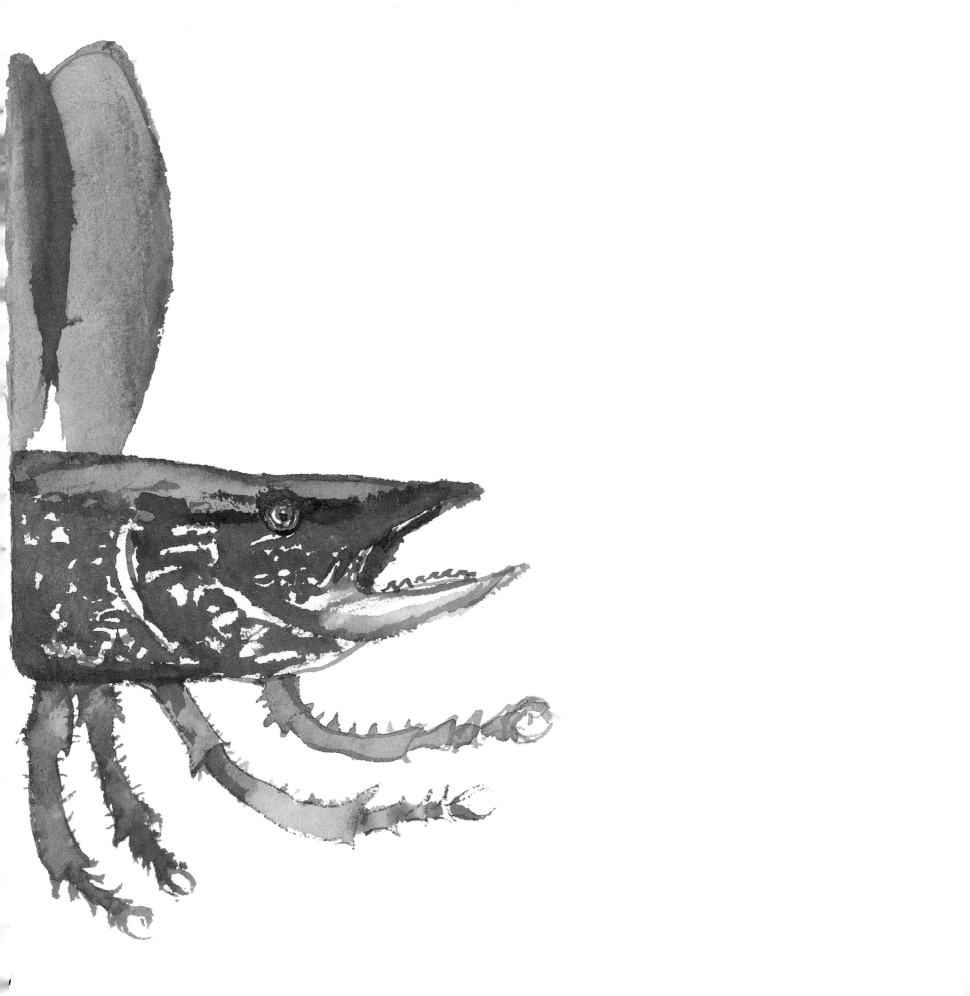

Fishflies are neither fish nor flies, but all have four multi-veined wings and belong to the insect club called Neuroptera. These insects are weak fliers who spend their childhood (as larvae) underwater, living under rocks in streams, where they serve as food for many freshwater fish. Those that grow up hang out near home, and are often caught and used as fish bait.

There really are flying fish, however. Some have two wings and some have four. The wings are really enlarged, colorful fins, but fish do not have the proper muscles to flap their "wings." Instead they swim at speeds up to 40 miles per hour toward the water's surface, spread their fins as they enter the air, and glide back down, landing with a splash.

Robber Fly

My math homework is missing!
So's Dad's twenty-dollar bill!
And Mom can't find the cake left cooling
on the windowsill.

I didn't eat it!
Spend it!
Or forget that it was due!

It must have been . . .

a robber fly.

Why would I lie to you?

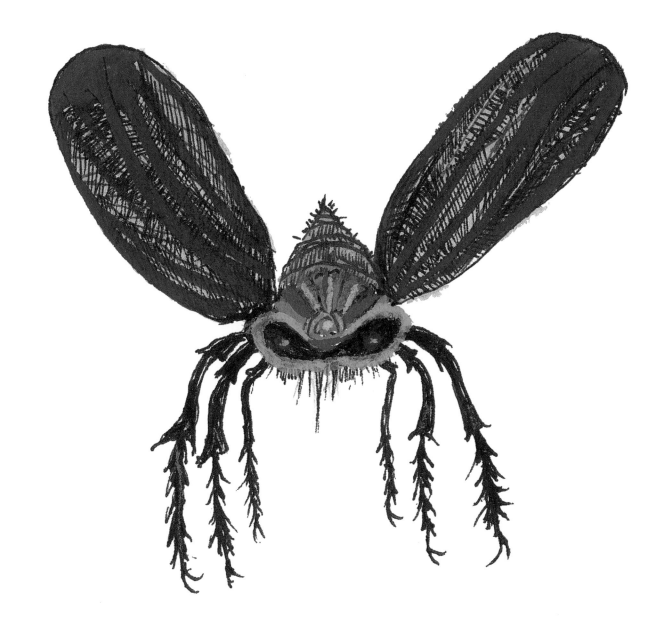

Robber flies, also known as assassin flies, suck the blood of their prey. Like horseflies, they are large (often over an inch long) but unlike their relatives, they attack only other insects, and can help control pests. (Insect pests, not your brothers and sisters.) They have bristly mustaches and beards, and their bulging eyes are huge.

Robber flies are hairy, like spiders. They also have yellow and black abdomens, like bees, whom they pretend to befriend, and then attack. Mostly though, they're bullies who pick on smaller insects. They wait for them to pass by and then leap on their backs, robbing their prey of their most precious possession—life.

There is no honor among these thieves. A male robber fly's most dangerous enemy is the female robber fly, who is as likely to *kill* her mate, as to *mate*.

House Fly

I wish my house could fly. Here's why: the clock says ten till eight.
My hair's uncombed,
    my teeth unbrushed,
        and I don't feel so great.
I hate to hurry but Mom is worried that the bus won't wait.
School starts in minutes. I'll be half an hour late!

If houses flew like house flies do, Mom wouldn't have to shout.
I'd yawn,
  and stretch,
    and brush,
      and comb,
        and lollygag about.
I'd disembark before the bus could park. And then, no doubt,
my house would come to fly me home again when school is out.

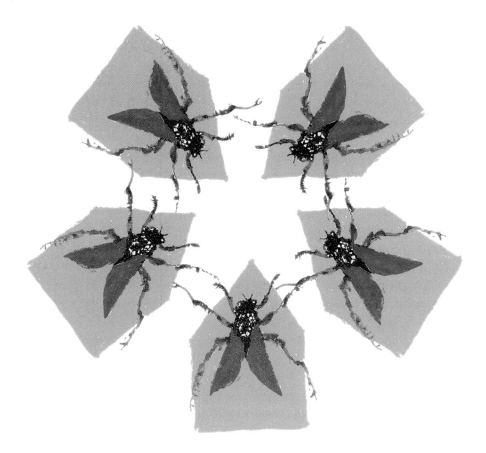

Not all flies in your house are *House flies*. Some are just passing through, or lost. A real housefly lives in your home, flying about the rooms and walking over the walls and ceilings (the tip of each foot has a pair of claws and two pads; the entire foot is covered with tiny hairs that have a sticky solution at their tips).

House flies don't have teeth and they can't bite. If you're home and a fly bites you, don't blame the house fly. Neither do house flies taste with their mouths. They taste with their feet, walking around until they touch exposed food, at which point a short tube automatically descends and, like a vacuum cleaner, sucks up the nutrients.

Deer Fly

My Dad's a mighty hunter.
He's a he-man type of guy.
I hate to brag but once he bagged
a bloodthirsty deer fly.

He strapped it to the rooftop
of his macho, souped-up Dodge,
and now it's stuffed and mounted
in   the

DEERFLY

HUNTER'S

LODGE

42

A **_Deer fly_** is similar to a horse fly, but smaller, and generally a more colorful brown and yellow. What it lacks in size, however, it makes up for in persistence. Deer flies feed on blood, circling rapidly around their victims before biting them painfully.

Deer love the woods and deer flies love deer, so it is not uncommon for these flies also to annoy campers. Get close enough and you will notice that deer flies often have brilliant green or golden eyes with zigzag stripes. The colors, unfortunately, fade after death, so you need to look before you slap.

Latrine Fly

A "cowpie" was my birthing place,
that's why I have a dirty face.
My classmates call me "stinkerbell,"
but I love *all* of nature's smells.

Even college-educated
flies know soap is overrated.
I take my showers in the sewer
and snack for hours on horse manure.

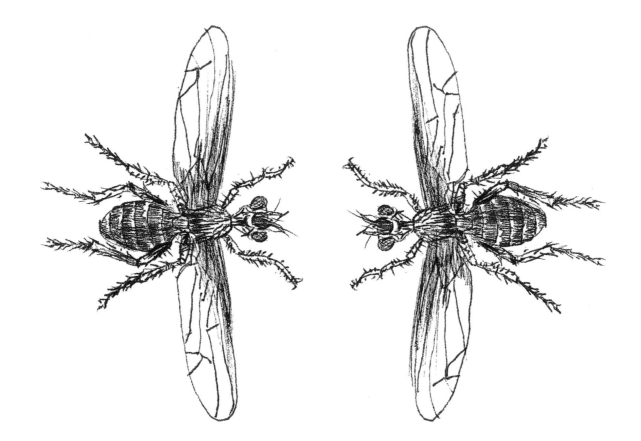

Latrine flies really do lay their eggs in horse and cow droppings. While this might sound yucky to you, it makes sense for flies, ensuring a safe (you'd stay away) and moist place for youngsters to grow up in. While the nutritional value is low, excrement is an excellent breeding ground for bacteria, which are food for baby latrine flies.

Male latrine flies will hang out around the freshest piles of dung that they can find, knowing that the hairy yellow female latrine fly will eventually fly by to lay eggs. What a way to find a girlfriend!

Coffin Fly

Humans are foolish.
They think that it's ghoulish
to try on shrouds and coffins.

They'll size their socks
but not the box
their loved ones see them off in.

A fly instead
will think ahead
and buy a comfy final bed.

Funerals don't make me nervous.
I'll rest in peace
throughout my service.

Coffin flies live their lives in buried coffins, feeding on dead bodies. YUCK! There's a bad joke that goes, "People are dying to get into their coffins." Nobody knows how the coffin flies get into closed coffins. They are the magicians of flies. Flying is no longer necessary for these tiny insects, so they have evolved tiny wings and weak flight muscles, but somehow they manage to dig through the soil, breathing what little air they can find, and they live their complete life underground, in the subterranean dark.

Fairyfly

We never bite.
We're erudite,
polite,
and pulchritudinous.
(That means we're pretty,
witty,
wise,
without a mood
that's rude in us.)

We're perfect hosts.
We never boast
(almost),
thieve, cuss,
or even fuss.
We have no vices,
we're so nice, is
why kids
disbelieve in us.

You don't believe in *Fairyflies*? You've never seen one? Maybe that's because fairyflies are the smallest of all the insects. They are so tiny that they are smaller than the period at the end of this sentence.

Fairyflies are not really flies. They are tiny wasps (they belong to the club Hymenoptera), and as small as they are, they still have four wings, which they use like paddles to swim underwater in search of dragonfly eggs, inside of which they lay their own, even tinier eggs.

To
L.B.
from
R.M.

To
R.M.
from
L.B.

Text copyright © 1999 by Richard Michelson.
Illustrations copyright © 1999 by Leonard Baskin.
All rights reserved
Marshall Cavendish, 99 White Plains Road, Tarrytown, NY 10591

Library of Congress Cataloging-in-Publication Data
Michelson, Richard. A book of flies real or otherwise/ by Richard Michelson; illustrated by Leonard Baskin.
p.   cm. Summary: Humorous poems about different kinds of flies are accompanied by factual
information about these creatures.
ISBN 0-7614-5050-5   1. Flies—Juvenile poetry. 2. Children's poetry, American.
[1. Flies—Poetry. 2. American poetry.] I. Baskin, Leonard, date, ill. II. Title.
PS3563.I34B66   1999   811'.54—dc21   98-46894   CIP   AC

Printed in Hong Kong   First Edition   6   5   4   3   2   1

56